Contents

The daredevil businessman

Richard says: "I love to experience as much as I can of life. The physical adventures I have been involved in have added a special dimension to my life that has reinforced the pleasure I take in my business."

WOW!

As well as sailing and ballooning, the daredevil businessman has a go at skiing, skydiving and bungee jumping.

Richard won the British record for crossing the Atlantic on the Virgin Atlantic Challenger II *in 1986.*

Richard Branson is one of the richest men in the world. He has a loving wife and family. He even owns a Caribbean island. He heads one of the most successful and famous group of companies in the world. But, the man who has it all would risk it all in a moment. Richard has taken part in some of the most dangerous challenges at sea or in the air. In 1985 he hit the headlines when his powerboat *Virgin Atlantic*

In 1998 Richard attempted an around-the-world flight in his hot-air balloon. Unfortunately, he had to be rescued from the Pacific Ocean on Christmas day.

Challenger sank during an attempt to make the fastest Atlantic Ocean crossing by boat. Richard had to be rescued by an RAF helicopter. A year later he broke the record in the *Atlantic Challenger II*.

Next Richard took to the skies in a balloon. In 1987 he flew from England to New England, USA. He made the journey in record-breaking time. In 1997 the balloon he aimed to fly around the world crash landed in the Sahara desert. The following year Richard attempted the record again. This time his team broke the record for an air balloon flight from Morocco to Hawaii. Richard's adventures can be likened to his life in business. He always aims for the top. If he fails then he will try and try again to achieve his goal!

HONOURS BOARD

Some of the companies within the Virgin empire:

Virgin Books, Virgin Vision, Top Nosh food, Virgin Rags, Virgin Pubs, Virgin Coke, Virgin Brides, Heaven nightclub, Virgin Condoms, Virgin Vie and Virgin Media.

Childhood challenges

Where did Richard Branson get his spirit for adventure? How did he get his independence and **self-belief**? Richard thanks his parents. He believes their love and encouragement set him up for becoming a successful businessman.

TOP TIP

"A good company runs as if it is a family. If your son messes up, you don't kick him out of the house." Richard Branson, on how to deal with employees that make a mistake.

In 2006 Richard attended a film premiere party with his parents, Ted and Eve.

Richard was born on 18 July 1950 in Blackheath, London. His father Ted was a barrister and his mother Eve an air steward. Richard has two sisters Vanessa and Lindi. The family moved to the village of Shamley Green in Surrey when Richard was a young boy. Richard spent much of his early years playing outdoors in the surrounding countryside. When he was about five he learned to swim in a river. When the current pulled him down he nearly drowned, but he kicked to the surface and realised he could swim.

Richard's family was quite comfortable but they weren't rich. His mother was always coming up with new money-making schemes. From a young age Richard was expected to help her. As well as being **resourceful** Eve expected her children to be independent. When Richard was four she dropped him off a few miles from home. He was supposed to find his own way back cutting through the fields. He ended up getting lost. At 12 Richard cycled fifty miles to Bournemouth. He says that completing the challenge made him feel like a hero!

INSPIRATION

Richard says that his family is the most important thing to him: "I cannot remember a moment in my life when I have not felt the love of my family. We were a family that would have killed for each other – and we still are."

Richard celebrated his record for the fastest Atlantic Ocean crossing with the Prime Minister, Margaret Thatcher.

School days

Richard was eight when he was sent away to Scaitcliffe School in Windsor Park. He hated being away from home. He also struggled with **dyslexia** and poor vision. As a result he didn't perform well academically. Fortunately, he was good at sport and was captain of the school cricket and football teams.

The headmaster of Stowe once said: "Congratulations, Branson. I predict that you will either go to prison or become a millionaire."

WOW!

Richard believes that his dyslexia has helped him become more successful in business: "When I launch a new company, I need to understand the advertising. If I can understand it, then I believe anybody can."

Richard always looked forward to the holidays at home. When he was nine he dreamed up his first business idea. He planted Christmas trees on spare land owned by his parents. The plan was that by the time he was 18 and ready to leave school these trees would be fully grown. The money he raised from selling trees could be used to fund a trip to India. Unfortunately, rabbits ate the young Christmas trees!

Richard was nearly **expelled** from his next school, Cliff View House. When he became depressed his parents moved him to Stowe, a famous public school. A knee injury meant he couldn't play sport and he continued to get poor exam results.

Unhappy but determined to do something worthwhile he began writing a novel. He also wrote to the headmaster suggesting changes to the school rules. At 17 Richard decided to drop out of school without any qualifications.

From rebel school boy to knight. In 1999, Richard was awarded a knighthood for his 'services to entrepreneurship.'

The accidental entrepreneur

The 1960s was an exciting time to be a teenager. Bands like the Beatles and the Rolling Stones topped the charts. Flowery shirts, silver space age dresses and mini skirts were in fashion. On a more serious note, a war thousands of miles away in Vietnam was taking millions of lives. Richard did not like what was happening in the world and wanted to do something about it.

At the time there wasn't a magazine for young people that covered issues like the Vietnam War. Richard dreamed of setting up a magazine where interviews with **intellectuals** or politicians of the day were next to stories about rock stars and movie actors.

"I wanted to be an editor or a journalist, I wasn't really interested in being an entrepreneur, but I soon found I had to become an entrepreneur in order to keep my magazine going."

WOW!

Richard set up the magazine *Student* when he was at school. He didn't have any money other than the £4 his mother gave him for post and telephone charges. He was only 16 but he managed to sell over £5,000 of advertising to fund the magazine. The first edition was free because the advertising **revenue** met all the costs.

After he left school Richard moved to London and ran the magazine from a friend's basement. At times it was more like a party than work. Richard interviewed mega stars of the day like the Rolling Stones.

TOP TIP

"I keep a notebook in my pocket all the time and I really do listen to what people say, even when we're out in a club at 3 am and someone's passing on an idea. Good ideas come from people everywhere, not in the boardroom." Richard Branson

In the 1960s, Mick Jagger from the Rolling Stones spoke out against the current political circumstances.

Virgin is born

Richard loved music and he noticed that most of his friends did too. At the time record shops were expensive. A **mail-order** business was one way of keeping the prices down. In 1970 Richard started his own record mail order business. He thought about calling his new **venture** 'Slipped Disc'. Somebody in the office suggested 'Virgin Records'.

This was an unconventional name but it appealed to Richard's sense of humour. He also liked the name because he was new to business and it reflected that. Going with the brand name Virgin is a decision he has never regretted.

The Virgin brand name and logo has become one of the most recognisable in the world.

INSPIRATION

Richard says about his company: "We look for opportunities where we can offer something better, fresher, and more valuable, and we seize them. We often move into areas where the customer has traditionally received a poor deal, and where the competition is **complacent**."

Richard ran an advert for mail-order records in the final issue of *Student* magazine. When the magazine folded he concentrated on building up his record business. In 1970 he opened a small record shop in London's Notting Hill Gate. It was a place where customers could relax on beanbags and listen to their favourite tunes on head phones. There was also free vegetarian food and music papers.

A bigger store opened in Oxford Street, London in early 1971. Virgin record shops expanded throughout the UK in the 1970s. In 1979 Richard opened his first large-scale record shop, called the Virgin Megastore in London. Virgin Megastores opened all over the world, including America, Europe, Japan and the Middle East.

WOW!

Richard is a clever businessman and always looking at ways to save money. He didn't pay rent on his first record shop in Oxford Street, London. He convinced the landlord of the shop below that Virgin Records would attract a lot of people who would also shop at the landlord's shoe store.

The Virgin Megastore in Times Square, New York. When it first opened it was one of the largest music stores in the USA.

Recording in the countryside

In 1971 Richard had another new and exciting business idea. Why not make a luxurious recording studio in the countryside? At that time many studios were uncomfortable and had strict timetables. Richard wanted to make a place where musicians could relax and let their creative juices flow.

He found a beautiful old manor house in Oxfordshire that was up for sale. Unfortunately, he did not have the money to buy it. Many people would have walked away from the dream at that moment. Richard did not, and that's one of the secrets of his success. He managed to negotiate a cheaper price for the house and borrow money from his family.

In the 1970s, Richard enjoyed some wild times at the Manor Studio in Oxfordshire.

In 1971 Richard was enjoying an **unconventional** business life. He loved to party and did most of his business lying in bed or at a coffee table. The Manor became a place for wild parties. One day an unknown musician called Mike Oldfield walked through the doors. Record companies had turned him away because his music was too unusual. Richard decided to give him a chance.

Mike Oldfield spent over a year creating his masterpiece, the album *Tubular Bells*. It was daring because it had no vocals or drums. It became the first record to be released on the Virgin Records label. After its release in 1973 it stayed in the album charts for 279 weeks. It sold over 15 million copies worldwide and was the making of the Virgin Record label. The label went on to sign top acts such as the Rolling Stones, the Sex Pistols and Culture Club.

Tom Newman, one of the founders of the Manor Studio has said: "*Tubular Bells* made Virgin. But even if it hadn't happened in this way, Richard Branson would have made it in some other way."

WOW!

Richard Branson has named a Virgin America and Virgin Atlantic aircraft 'Tubular Belle'.

Richard Branson with Mike Oldfield at the launch of the Tubular Belle.

HONOURS BOARD

Bands that recorded at the Manor Studio:

Cast
Radiohead
Teenage Fanclub
INXS
Black Sabbath
Tangerine Dream

A day in the life of Richard Branson

Richard married girlfriend Kristen Tomassi in 1972. By now work was taking over his life. Richard blames the break-up of his first marriage on his business. It is a mistake he tried not to make when he met his future wife Joan Templeton in 1976. They had their first child, a girl called Holly, in 1981.

WOW!

Richard bought the uninhabited island of Necker in 1979. The owner wanted £3,000,000 but Richard snapped it up for £180,000.

Richard and Joan with their children, Holly and Sam.

Their son Sam was born in 1984. The couple finally got married in 1989. Though Richard is a self-confessed workaholic he spends his free time relaxing with his family. The weekends are spent at their home in Oxfordshire. In the summer they head to Richard's Caribbean island Necker. In the comfort of his own private paradise he can indulge in watersports, tennis and swimming. In the winter the family enjoy a break at their South African game reserve Ulusaba.

When you are the head of an enormous organisation like Virgin no two days are the same. Richard is bursting with energy and ready to leap into action any day of the week. Richard reckons he travels for 250 days a year. When he is in Britain he works from his London home during the week. He's more comfortable working at a coffee table or sitting in the armchair at the end of his living room than in an office. He writes everything down in a diary rather than using a computer. The unconventional businessman also uses a gym bag instead of a brief case. He gets up at 5am each day. By 6am he is already on the phone making international phone calls.

Today Necker is an exclusive holiday getaway for the Bransons and anybody rich enough to pay $53,000 (£33,000) per night for the island (for up to 28 guests).

WOW!

You can experience what Richard fits into his business day by going on the Internet and watching him on You Tube or following him on Twitter!

Virgin takes to the skies

One of Richard's most daring projects is Virgin Atlantic Airways. The new airline was founded in 1984. Many people thought it was mad to start a new airline offering flights between London and New York. They believed that large airlines such as British Airways would force it out of business. There were also the costs to consider. Rather than risk too much money on a venture that might not work Richard **leased** a second-hand Boeing 707-200. Richard also believed Virgin could offer something new to customers. With Virgin Atlantic he aimed to deliver the best for less.

Richard celebrates Virgin Atlantic's 25th birthday at Newark Airport in June 2009.

G-VFAB

Virgin Atlantic Airways is now more than 25 years old and is one of the most profitable and popular airlines in the business. It offers flights between the UK and the USA, Africa, Australia, the Middle East and Asia.

Richard believes Virgin has transformed air travel. Virgin was the first to introduce seat-back videos for each passenger and beds. The Virgin cabin crew not only look good in their red uniforms, they always remember to smile and have fun. It hasn't always been easy. In 1992 he had to sell the Virgin record label to keep the airline going. There has also been a long and costly **feud** with rival British Airways. Despite the downs, it has been up most of the way.

WOW!

Richard has dressed as a steward doing trolley service on a flight from London to New York! "I believe enormously that if you can get out and experience things first-hand, you can see where things are going wrong or make things go right."

Boarding Pass

Virgin atlantic

Passenger Name
BRANSON/RICHARDMR
To
FLY VIRGIN ROUND-THE-WORLD

V australia
Every day a new idea takes off

Route options
1 VIRGIN GLOBAL EAST: SYDNEY - LOS ANGELES - LONDON - HONG KONG - SYDNEY
2 VIRGIN GLOBAL WEST: SYDNEY - HONG KONG - LONDON - LOS ANGELES - SYDNEY

Airline	Flight	Class
VS	VS201	PREMIUM ECONOMY

Seat	Date	Boarding
1K	2009	NOW

Passenger Name
BRANSON/RICHARDMR
To
FLY VIRGIN ROUND-THE-WORLD

Airline	Flight	Class
VS	VS201	PREMIUM ECONOMY

Seat	Date	Boarding
1K	2009	NOW

Virgin atlantic
V australia
Every day a new idea takes off

In 2009, Virgin offered a round-the-world air ticket. Now passengers can travel around the world with one airline.

19

The publicity machine

"I realised early in life that to put Virgin on the map, I did not have ad budgets, so I'd have to use myself."

Richard found another way of lowering the costs of setting up Virgin Atlantic Airways. Advertising the airline was too expensive. He had to think of new ways of promoting the company. To make sure the new airline was in the news the first flight was filled with celebrities. Richard has also played a large part in promoting his companies. He regularly dresses up for publicity events. He has dressed up as everything from Elvis to a Zulu warrior in the name of publicity.

Richard is happy to dress up or strip off to promote Virgin! In 2006, he put on a Union Jack suit in Dubai, United Arab Emirates.

Richard has also exploited his love of adventure and dangerous sports to promote the Virgin brand. Every time he has attempted a land, air speed and distance record the famous red Virgin logo is prominently on display. Even when the record-breaking attempt has gone wrong it has meant publicity for the company.

In 1998 the US Coast Guard had to pluck Richard and his team from the sea when a balloon flight across the Pacific failed. When the story hit the headlines some people got angry. They did not think that one of the richest men in the world should use a public funded service. Richard gave a large contribution to the US Coast Guard.

HONOURS BOARD

Richard's record breakers:

1986: Richard crosses the Atlantic Ocean on the *Virgin Atlantic Challenger II* in the fastest recorded time.

1987: Richard flies a hot-air balloon across the Atlantic. *The Virgin Atlantic Flyer* is the largest balloon ever flown and reaches speeds of 209 km/h (130 miles per hour).

1991: Richard crosses the Pacific Ocean, from Japan to Arctic Canada in record time, breaking the record for distance. This time the balloon reaches speeds of 394 km/h (245 miles per hour).

1998: Richard Branson, Per Lindstrand and Steve Fossett made a record-breaking balloon flight from Morocco to Hawaii.

2004: Richard breaks the record for the fastest crossing of the English Channel by amphibious vehicle. The *Gibbs Aquada* makes the crossing in 1 hour, 40 minutes.

In 1989 Richard and pilot Per Lindstrand set off on their hot-air balloon flight across the Pacific.

Mind the gap!

In the early 1990s train travel in Britain was poor and unreliable. Many of British Rail's trains were old and scruffy. When the trains ran they never seemed to be on time. And, the food served up on the buffet cars was horrible. When British Rail was **privatised** in the mid-1990s Richard Branson was quick to jump on board the railway business.

Virgin Trains won two **franchises**: Intercity West Coast and Intercity Cross Country. Richard believed that they would be able to offer quicker, better and cheaper train travel. Little did Richard know, he was in for a bumpy ride.

WOW!

In 2009 Richard starred in a TV advert for Virgin Trains. He played the part of a tattooed rubbish collector.

Virgin Trains believe they can get you to your destination faster than any other trainline.

Richard wanted to bring train travel into the twenty-first century. In 1997 Virgin ordered £1 billion worth of new **rolling stock,** the largest order in British history. The order included super sleeker, faster, tilting trains called Pendolinos. Unfortunately, Virgin lost face with the public because there were delays in the delivery of the stock.

By 2004 Virgin had replaced all British Rail trains. However, British railway tracks were in need of modernisation. Virgin Trains could not go faster until the lines were updated.

In February 2007 a Pendolino train was derailed near Oxenholme, UK. Richard praised the driver of the train at the crash site and claimed the Pendolino was one of the safest trains. The same year Virgin Trains lost the Cross Country franchise. Virgin Trains has not lived up to its promise, but in 2009 more track upgrades means that they should now be able to provide better rail journeys.

TOP TIP

"Conventional wisdom says to specialise in one area and don't stray, and that the best businesses stick to their core ... But personally, I think rules are made to be broken." Richard Branson

Richard was very concerned when he faced the press after the 2007 derailment.

Changing the world

Richard has always wanted to change the world. Now he has the money and the reputation to make those changes. Richard's skill has been in setting up companies, not charities. He set up a non-profit condom company called Mates in the 1980s. It was his way of doing something to fight against AIDS.

In 2000 Richard really believed he could make a difference to people's lives by running the national lottery. He planned to take no profits from the People's Lottery so he could give more to charity. Eventually, Richard's People's Lottery lost out to the bid from Camelot. Losing the lottery bid was one of the biggest knocks to his career.

In recent years Richard has been more successful in his bid to change the world. In 2007 he set up the Virgin Earth Challenge. The competition has $25 million in prize money.

Richard and his son, Sam on an Arctic expedition in 2007. Sam was keeping a diary to record changes in temperature.

The winner must find a way to stop global warming. Richard has **pledged** to invest profits from his airline and train businesses for ten years to find new **green fuels**.

In 2007 Richard also helped to found the Elders. This independent group of elder statesmen, women and public figures includes Nelson Mandela, Kofi Annan, Mary Robinson, Desmond Tutu and Jimmy Carter. The group works to raise funds and discuss solutions for world issues such as war in the Middle East, poverty, AIDS and climate change. In August 2009 Richard joined the Elders on a trip to Israel to discuss the Israeli-Palestinian conflict.

WOW!

In May 2009 Richard took part in a three-day hunger strike to raise awareness of the suffering of people living through the war in Darfur.

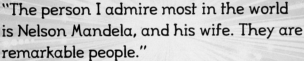

INSPIRATION

"The person I admire most in the world is Nelson Mandela, and his wife. They are remarkable people."

Richard with Nelson Mandela and wife Graca Machel at a launch for the anti-HIV and AIDS Campaign (2004).

The final frontier

Space has always been in Richard Branson's blood. In 1969 he remembers watching the first moon landing on a black and white television set in a London squat. In 1991 he registered the name Virgin Galactic. In 2005 a boyhood fantasy became reality when he teamed up with **aerospace** designer Burt Rutan. Together, they formed the Spacecraft Building Company.

This company designs and builds the rocket ships and tourist planes that Virgin Galactic will use in space. Richard is more than a little excited about the project. When he was asked what inspired him about space he replied: "Everything. The view, the weightlessness, the sheer majesty of it. I love to do things I've never done before. It's certainly the biggest thing Virgin's ever done... and it's my biggest adventure."

Virgin Galactic space crafts. Richard has said that there might be a reality show where the first prize is a seat on the first flight into space.

Virgin Galactic promises to send the first paying passengers on a **sub-orbital spaceflight**. Tickets will cost about £150,000 per person. The space tourists will go on a three-hour journey, 109 km (68 miles) above the Earth. They will be able to see the curvature of the Earth and look 1, 609 km (1,000 miles) in any direction. Then, for about four minutes, they will be able to take off their seatbelts and experience weightlessness.

Test flights have taken place at the Mojave Air and Space Port in California, USA. Richard hopes the first flight will take place within the next two years. Richard and Burt Rutan plan to be on the first flight along with Richard's parents, wife and children. Richard believes that in the future there will be orbital flights and a Virgin Hotel just off the moon.

WOW!

Richard reckons the same technology for space travel can be used to reduce the times of air travel. One day he thinks it will be possible to travel from New York to Sydney, Australia in 2.5 hours, rather than 26 hours.

Richard wants people to be able to get married in space!

The impact of Richard Branson

Sir Richard Branson is probably Britain's best-known entrepreneur. He founded Virgin in 1970 and controls or has stakes in more than 285 Virgin companies. The *Sunday Times* Rich List in 2009 ranked him the 32nd richest person in Britain. The Forbes' 2009 list of billionaires claims he is the 261st richest person in the world.

Richard is worth anything between £1,200 million and £1,500 million, although he is difficult to value. Many successful business people have money behind them. Richard started out with very little and this inspires people today.

Richard always flies the flag. He's proud to be British and never tires of promoting the Virgin brand.

Richard has many secrets for success. First, business has to be fun. Next, he's trusted and well-liked. People like him because he isn't a typical businessman. In the past he's turned up at important meetings with odd shoes or barefoot. Richard always appears laid-back but he enjoys the cut and thrust of the business world. However, he doesn't like the business boardroom. He prefers to follow his own instincts. New ideas are more likely to come to him while he's out and about rather than in a stuffy office. Virgin employees call him Dr Yes because he's so open to new suggestions. The Virgin website welcomes new ideas from would-be entrepreneurs.

Richard also likes a challenge. People thought he was mad when he started the airline business. Richard won't take no for an answer and now wants to send people into space. It is anybody's guess what Richard will do next. One thing is for sure, he's having too much fun to think about retiring!

WOW!

Richard backed a winner in 2009 when he agreed to sponsor the Brawn GP team. In October Brawn GP team member, Jenson Button became Formula One World Champion for 2009.

Richard says:
"Fantasising about the future is one of my favourite pastimes."

Have you got what it takes to be an entrepreneur? Try this!

1) Do you have the knack of getting what you want?
a) Yes, I'm a go-getter.
b) I try but only get what I want sometimes.
c) No. I'm quiet and never push myself forward.

2) Have you got a winning business idea?
a) Yes, I can't wait to set up my first business.
b) Yes, but I'm too young to be an entrepreneur.
c) Business? Me? You must be joking.

3) Are you good with money?
a) Yes, I work part-time and save a little each month.
b) I like to earn money but I love to spend it.
c) No. I'm only good at spending money.

4) Does the business world excite you?
a) Yes. I'm learning the ropes in my part-time job.
b) Yes, stories about young entrepreneurs are a real inspiration.
c) No. It's boring!

5) Are you a risk-taker?
a) Yes. I have total self-belief!
b) I'll only take a risk if I secretly think I can do it.
c) No, risks are far too stressful.

6) If you have a good idea what are you going to do about it?
a) Talk to my parents, get some financial advice and make a business plan.
b) I have an idea but I need more time to think about it.
c) Nothing!

RESULTS

Mostly As: You seem to have a number of qualities that a entrepreneur needs! You're never too young to start up a business so get cracking today!

Mostly Bs: You have the potential to be an entrepreneur. First of all, you need to build your confidence in the workplace. Then you need to find a business idea that really gets you going.

Mostly Cs: Business is not for you – yet! Perhaps when you are older and have to earn your own living you may change your mind.

Glossary

aerospace   The technology for travelling in the earth's atmosphere or outer space.

complacent   Pleased with oneself or self-satisfied.

dyslexia   A condition which makes it difficult to read and spell.

entrepreneurship   The act of being an entrepreneur. An entrepreneur is someone who starts off their own business or enterprise and takes on responsibility for the risks and the outcome.

expelled   To be asked to leave a school permanently. Pupils can be expelled from school for continual bad behaviour.

feud   An ongoing argument between two individuals or any groups of people including companies or families.

franchise   To acquire the right to be an independent arm of a particular business.

green fuels   Alternative fuels to fossil fuels such as coal and oil. Also known as biofuels, green fuels include liquid fuels made from plant materials.

intellectual   Someone who is intelligent and thoughtful.

leased   To pay to borrow or use something belonging to another person for an agreed length of time.

mail-order   To buy goods to be sent out by post rather than buy them at a shop.

pledge   A solemn promise to do something.

privatised   A private company is owned by an individual or a group of people called shareholders. Nationalised companies are state-owned and controlled by the government. If a nationalised company is sold to business people or into the private sector then it is called a 'privatised company.'

resourceful   To be clever at thinking up better ways of doing things or making money.

revenue   Money that comes into a business from the sale of goods or services.

rolling stock   The locomotives, carriages and other vehicles used on a railway.

self-belief   Confidence in your self and your own abilities.

sub-orbital spaceflight   To fly into space but not make a full orbit of the earth.

unconventional   Describes a person who does not do things in the normal social manner. An unconventional person is likely to break the rules and do things in an original way.

venture   A risky enterprise or daring new business.

Index